PRIMARY BOOK 2

AZTEC MATH

John H. Lettau

**Small Deeds Done Are Better
Than Great Deeds Planned**

Fascinating New Approach Worksheets

TABLE OF CONTENTS

Introduction

AZTEC MATH PRIMARY 2 is a fascinating way to teach many mathematics concepts to grades 2 & 3. All worksheets are designed to teach a specific skill and at the same time create more interest in assigned worksheets.

AZTEC MATH PRIMARY 2 has several uses: (1) basic work for grades 2 &3 (2) enrichment work for grade 1 plus (3) remedial work for grades 4, 5 & 6.

All worksheets have "easy to follow" directions. Correction is also a simple task because of the colored design when to assignment is complete.

Encourage students to select their own color combinations when possible.

Reproduction permission is granted to individual teachers for classroom use.

More Primary Aztec Math worksheets can be found in BOOK ONE.

LARGER AND SMALLER

Color section ◯ when it contains ▢

Color section ◯ when it contains ◻

CIRCLES AND SQUARES

When the shape is a square - color ⬭

When the shape is a circle - color ◯

GEOMETRIC SHAPES

When the section contains a ◇ - color ⬭⬭

When the section contains a △ - color ⬭⬭

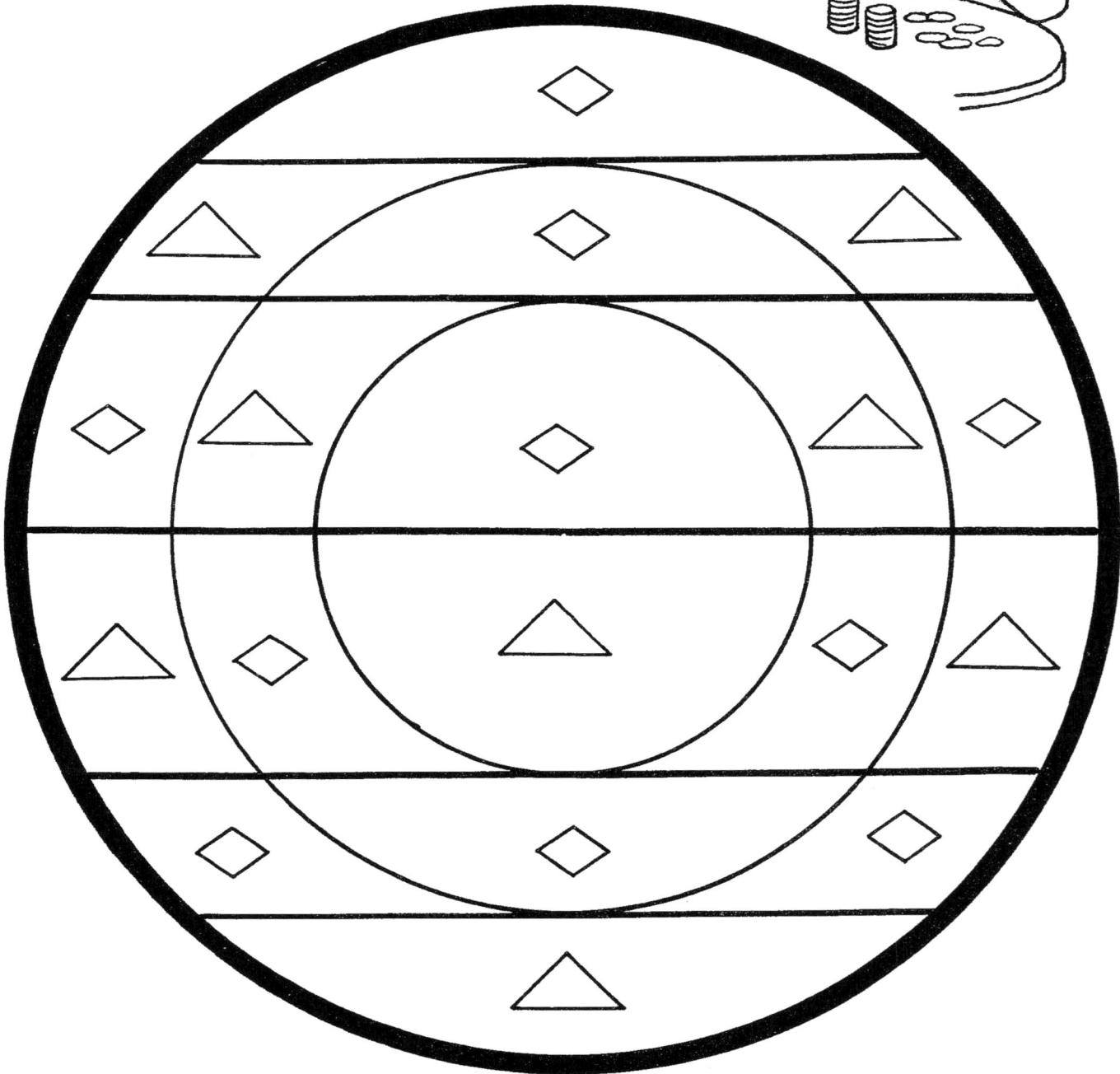

6

GEOMETRIC SHAPES

Color ⬭ when section contains a square ☐ .

Color ⬭ when section contains a circle ◯ .

Color ⬭ when section contains a triangle △ .

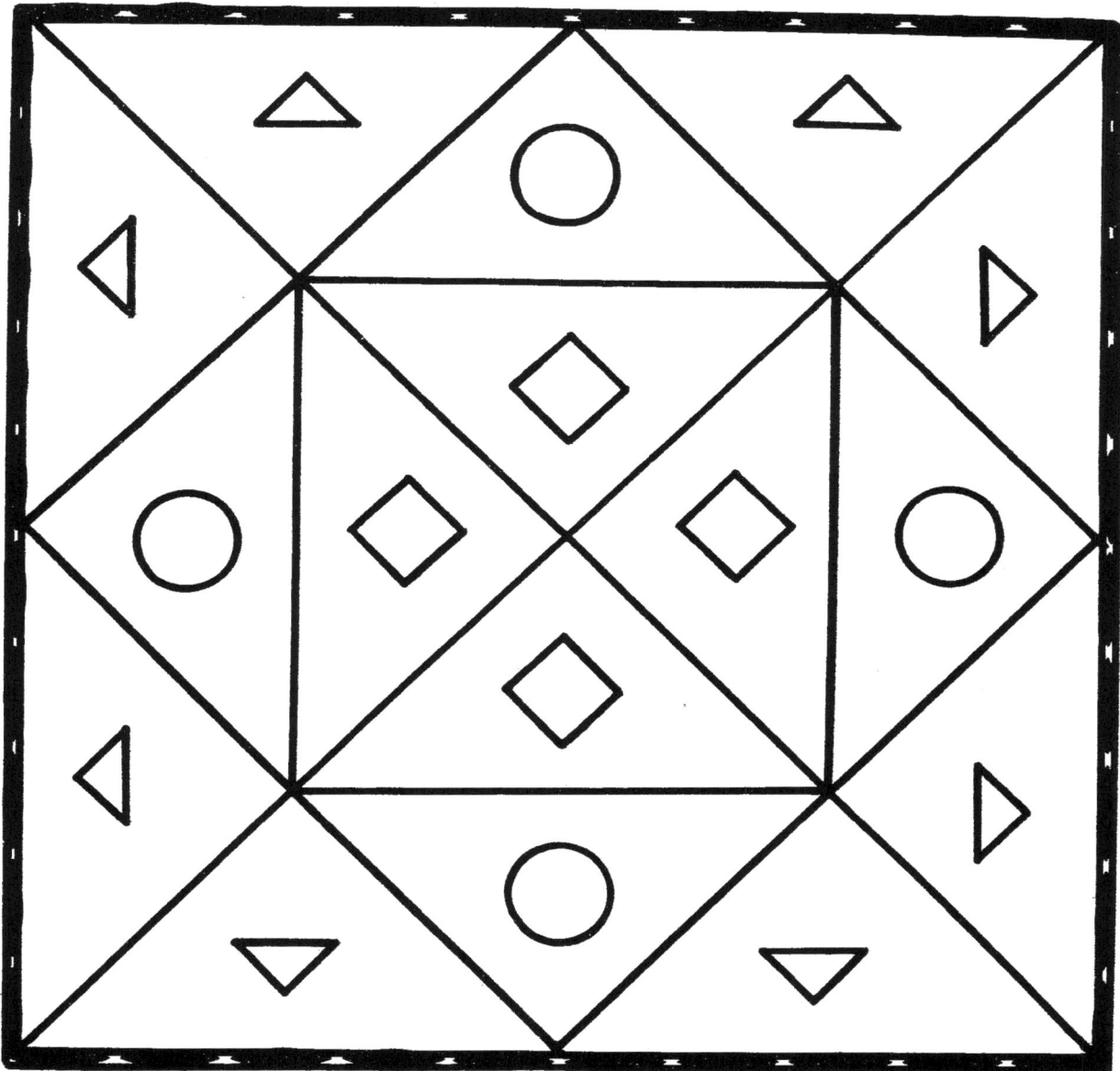

7

SETS

- ⬭ Color all sets of 1
- ⬭ Color all sets of 2
- ⬭ Color all sets of 3
- ⬭ Color all sets of 4

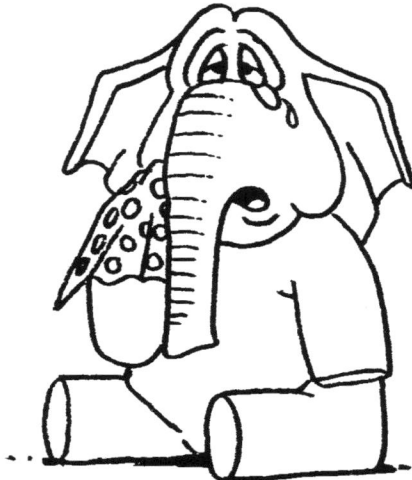

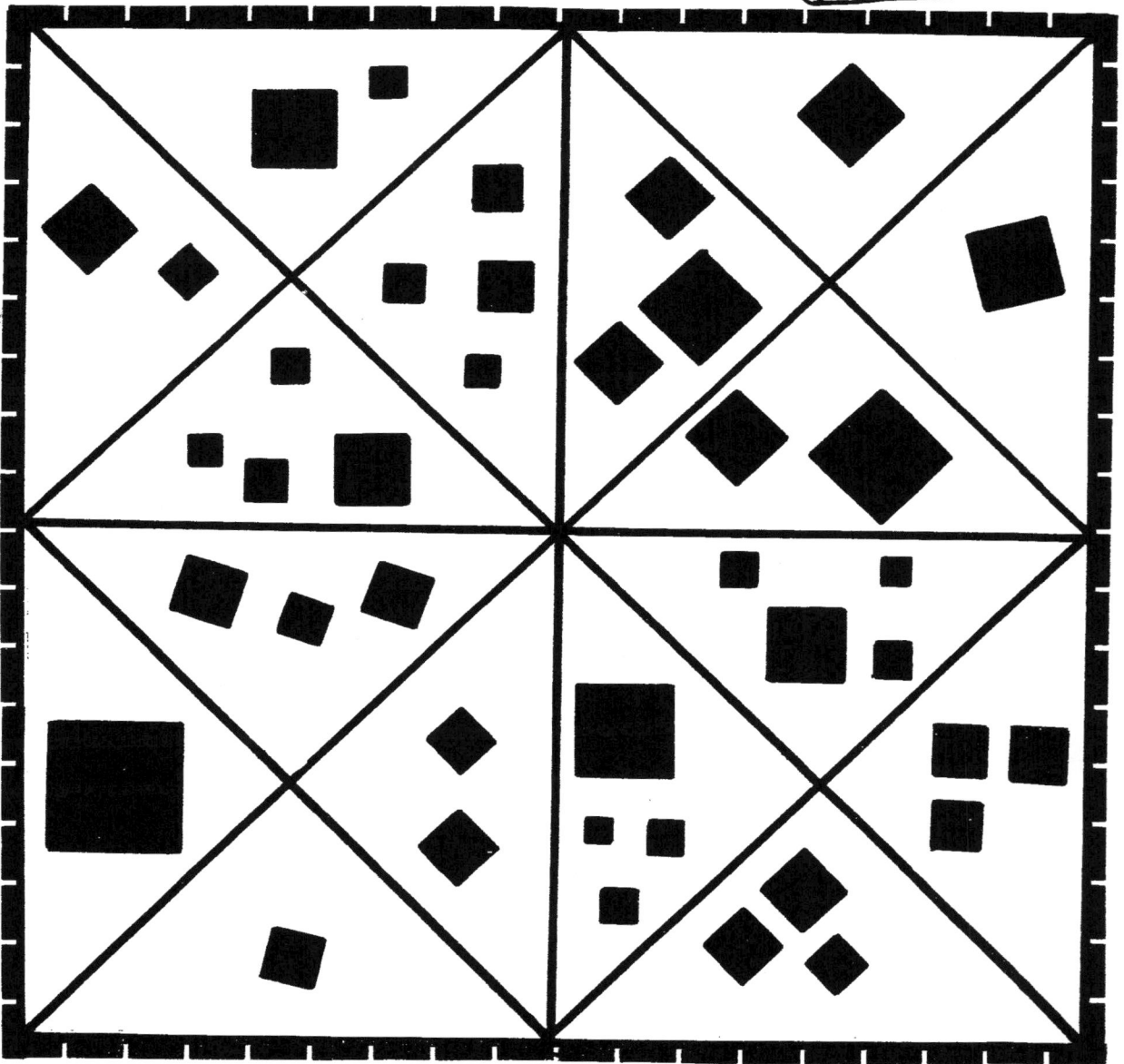

8

SETS

When the section contains a set of 1 - color ◯

When the section contains a set of 2 - color ◯

When the section contains a set of 3 - color ◯

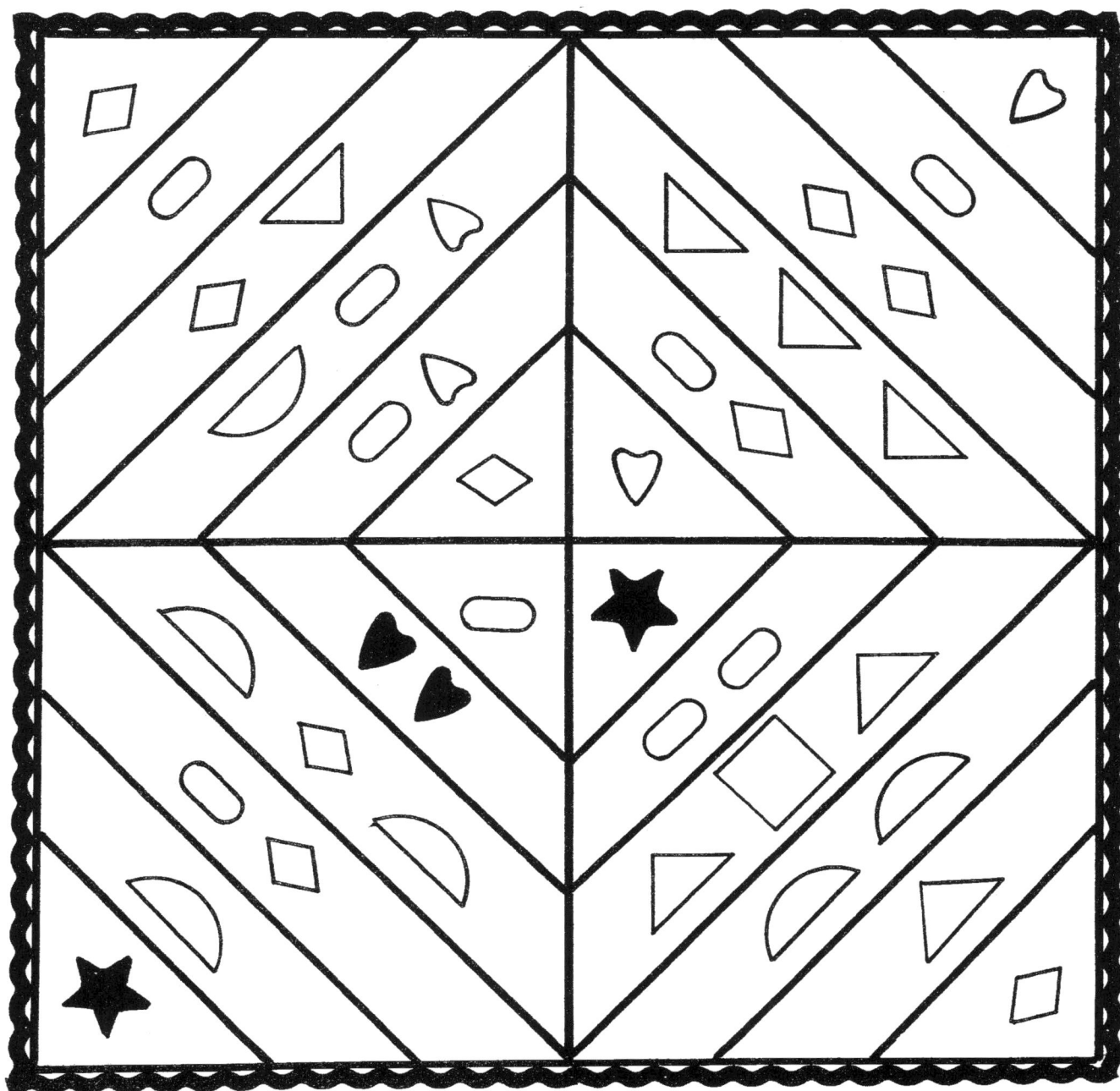

GREATER THAN — LESS THAN

Place < or > in each ⬭ .

If the sign is > - greater than.

If the sign is < - less than.

3 ⬭ 5   6 ⬭ 7   9 ⬭ 5   4 ⬭ 0

4 ⬭ 3   5 ⬭ 3   9 ⬭ 10   4 ⬭ 8

0 ⬭ 3   7 ⬭ 9   8 ⬭ 3   10 ⬭ 7

7 ⬭ 5   6 ⬭ 1   6 ⬭ 10   4 ⬭ 9

5 ⬭ 9   3 ⬭ 7   3 ⬭ 0   1 ⬭ 0

8 ⬭ 6   7 ⬭ 3   6 ⬭ 9   7 ⬭ 10

10 ⬭ 11   9 ⬭ 10   3 ⬭ 1   10 ⬭ 7

GREATER THAN & LESS THAN

Place either < or > in each square.

When < is in the square - color ◯

When > is in the square - color ◯

9 ☐ 6   5 ☐ 3

2 ☐ 1   6 ☐ 2

7 ☐ 2   1 ☐ 0   13 ☐ 15   3 ☐ 1   4 ☐ 6

5 ☐ 6   8 ☐ 10

2 ☐ 6   6 ☐ 4   0 ☐ 1   11 ☐ 7   2 ☐ 3

8 ☐ 7   10 ☐ 9

11 ☐ 8   10 ☐ 4

11

GREATER THAN and LESS THAN

Write < or < in each ◯.

When the missing sign is < , color ◯

When the missing sign is > , color ◯

17 ◯ 71   13 ◯ 31   200 ◯ 199   156 ◯ 155

78 ◯ 76   100 ◯ 200   212 ◯ 221   101 ◯ 100

91 ◯ 87   63 ◯ 60   310 ◯ 331   88 ◯ 89

251 ◯ 271   56 ◯ 51   131 ◯ 120   171 ◯ 272

361 ◯ 371   101 ◯ 111   69 ◯ 60   188 ◯ 180

44 ◯ 34   161 ◯ 191   81 ◯ 181   13 ◯ 11

283 ◯ 183   301 ◯ 300   73 ◯ 137   11 ◯ 101

19 ◯ 91   274 ◯ 234   313 ◯ 211   51 ◯ 151

17 ◯ 71   20 ◯ 22   95 ◯ 91   80 ◯ 60

12

TELLING TIME

If the time shown is correct color ◯

If the time shown is wrong color ◯

25 minutes to 7

10 minutes to 7

10 minutes to 2

10 minutes to 11

25 minutes to 6

25 minutes to 4

5 minutes to 10

25 minutes to 7

20 minutes to 1

TELLING TIME

Color section ☐ when time shown is correct.

Color section ☐ when time shown is incorrect.

12 o'clock

6 o'clock

4 o'clock

7 o'clock

4 o'clock

9 o'clock

4 o'clock

8 o'clock

11 o'clock

TELLING TIME

If the time shown is correct - color ⭕

If the time shown is wrong - color ⬭

30 minutes to 3	30 minutes to 5	30 minutes to 8
30 minutes to 12	30 minutes to 10	30 minutes to 8
30 minutes to 4	30 minutes to 11	30 minutes to 2

TELLING TIME

If the time shown is wrong - color ⬤

If the time shown is correct - color ⬤

26 minutes to 10	17 minutes after 3	16 minutes after 2
21 minutes after 12	23 minutes to 11	12 minutes after 5
14 minutes to 2	13 minutes after 9	1 minute to 7

ADDITION — SUMS 5 to 8

Color all sections with a sum of 5 ⬭
Color all sections with a sum of 6 ⬭
Color all sections with a sum of 7 ⬭
Color all sections with a sum of 8 ⬭

$3+2=$	$5+2=$ $3+2+2=$ $4+3=$ $1+6=$		$3+1+1=$
$4+4=$	$1+2+3=$		$3+5=$
$1+7=$ $3+3=$	$2+4=$ $5+1=$ $1+1+4=$ $2+2+2=$		$0+6=$ $7+1=$
$5+2+1=$	$0+2+4=$		$2+6=$
$4+1=$	$5+1+1=$ $1+2+4=$ $6+0+1=$ $4+3=$		$0+5=$

17

ADDITION — SUMS 6 to 9

Color section ☐ when sum is 6.

Color section ☐ when sum is 7.

Color section ☐ when sum is 8.

Color section ☐ when sum is 9.

3+3+1=	$\begin{array}{r}1\\2\\+3\\\hline\end{array}$	$\begin{array}{r}4\\1\\+1\\\hline\end{array}$	3+3+3=	$\begin{array}{r}1\\5\\+1\\\hline\end{array}$ $\begin{array}{r}3\\2\\+2\\\hline\end{array}$
2+3+2=			7+1+1=	

$\begin{array}{r}1\\1\\+4\\\hline\end{array}$ $\begin{array}{r}3\\1\\+2\\\hline\end{array}$

4+1+2=

5+1+1=

$\begin{array}{r}1\\2\\+4\\\hline\end{array}$ $\begin{array}{r}2\\4\\+1\\\hline\end{array}$

6+2+1=

5+3+1=

2+1+3=

2+2+2=

$\begin{array}{r}5\\2\\+1\\\hline\end{array}$ $\begin{array}{r}4\\2\\+2\\\hline\end{array}$

4+3+1=

6+1+1=

$\begin{array}{r}4\\3\\+2\\\hline\end{array}$ $\begin{array}{r}1\\6\\+2\\\hline\end{array}$

$\begin{array}{r}1\\6\\+1\\\hline\end{array}$ $\begin{array}{r}1\\4\\+3\\\hline\end{array}$

3+0+3=

1+4+1=

$\begin{array}{r}2\\4\\+3\\\hline\end{array}$ $\begin{array}{r}3\\1\\+5\\\hline\end{array}$

2+4+2=

2+5+1=

18

ADDITION — SUMS 10 to 13

When the sum is 10 - color ⬭
When the sum is 11 - color ⬭
When the sum is 12 - color ⬭
When the sum is 13 - color ⬭

3+4+4=	2+3+7=	9+1+1=

| $\begin{array}{r}6\\5\\+1\end{array}$ | $\begin{array}{r}8\\2\\+1\end{array}$ | 6+2+5= | | | $\begin{array}{r}4\\4\\+3\end{array}$ | $\begin{array}{r}3\\3\\+6\end{array}$ |

| 3+2+6= | | $\begin{array}{r}3\\5\\+2\end{array}$ | $\begin{array}{r}2\\8\\+1\end{array}$ | $\begin{array}{r}4\\2\\+4\end{array}$ | 6+0+5= | |

| $\begin{array}{r}4\\7\\+1\end{array}$ | $\begin{array}{r}5\\5\\+1\end{array}$ | | | | $\begin{array}{r}3\\1\\+7\end{array}$ | $\begin{array}{r}7\\2\\+3\end{array}$ |

| | 7+2+4= | |

| 5+2+4= | 5+2+5= | 4+2+5= |

19

ADDITION — SUMS 15 to 19

Color all sections with sums of 15 ☐.
Color all sections with sums of 16 ☐.
Color all sections with sums of 17 ☐.
Color all sections with sums of 18 ☐.
Color all sections with sums of 19 ☐.

$10 + 9 =$

$11 + 8 =$

$12 + 6 =$

$8 + 9 =$

$10 + 8 =$

$10 + 7 =$

$\begin{array}{r} 7 \\ +12 \\ \hline \end{array}$

$\begin{array}{r} 10 \\ +9 \\ \hline \end{array}$

$4 + 4 + 10 =$

$2 + 9 + 7 =$

$5 + 5 + 6 =$

$8 + 8 =$

$8 + 8 =$

$10 + 6 =$

$10 + 5 =$

$7 + 9 =$

$5 + 11 =$

$7 + 3 + 6 =$

$4 + 12 =$

$6 + 6 + 6 =$

$5 + 5 + 8 =$

$\begin{array}{r} 13 \\ +6 \\ \hline \end{array}$

$\begin{array}{r} 8 \\ 1 \\ +10 \\ \hline \end{array}$

$6 + 11 =$

$9 + 9 =$

$5 + 12 =$

$11 + 7 =$

$5 + 5 + 9 =$

$7 + 3 + 9 =$

20

ADDITION — SUMS 10 to 19

Color all sections with sums of 10 or 11 ⬭
Color all sections with sums of 12 or 13 ⬭⬭
Color all sections with sums of 14 or 15 ⬭⬭⬭⬭
Color all sections with sums of 16 or 17 ⬭⬭
Color all sections with sums of 18 or 19 ⬭

5+5=	6+7=	5+8=	7+7=
	9+7= 8+8=	7+10= 12+5=	
6+8=	10+3=	4+9=	6+4=
9+9=	12+7=	10+9=	6+12=
12+0= 1+12=			3+9= 7+5=
9+2=	4+7=	9+5=	6+8=
7+8=	4+10=	8+3=	0+11=
13+0= 9+4=			2+10= 5+8=
15+3=	14+4=	16+2=	18+1=
10+1=	0+13=	8+5=	9+6=
	13+3= 0+16=	17+0= 5+11=	
10+5=	7+6=	3+10=	4+6=

21

ADDITION — SUMS 17 to 19

Color all sections ☐ when the sum is 17.

Color all sections ☐ when the sum is 18.

Color all sections ☐ when the sum is 19.

$12 + 5$

$14 + 4$

$11 + 4 + 2$

$2 + 13 + 3$

$13 + 4$

$6 + 12$

$10 + 8$

$4 + 1 + 13$

$17 + 1$

$6 + 10 + 3$

$10 + 5 + 2 + 1$

$11 + 2 + 5 + 1$

$11 + 3 + 2 + 1$

$10 + 4 + 3$

$12 + 7$

$3 + 16$

$6 + 2 + 10$

$4 + 4 + 10$

$10 + 2 + 6$

$16 + 2$

$14 + 3$

$11 + 7$

$7 + 3 + 0 + 7$

$15 + 3$

$3 + 12 + 2$

ADDITION — SUMS TO 19

Work each problem. Circle the number in the one's place.

If the circled number is 0 or 1 - color ◯

If the circled number is 2, 3, or 4 - color ◯

If the circled number is 5 or 6 - color ◯

If the circled number is 7, 8, or 9 - color ◯

5 +5	7 +6	11 +5	10 6 +3	9 2 +4	2 10 +1	9 +2
8 +5	7 +4	9 +9	8 +8	4 9 +5	5 +6	9 +5
1 +0	7 +7	3 2 +0	6 12 +1	9 +6	6 3 +3	0 +0
6 5 +3	7 +3	13 +5	7 8 +1	9 8 +2	4 +6	4 5 +4

ADDITION OF TENS

Work each problem!

If the answer is 10, 20, or 30 - color ⬭

If the answer is 40, 50, or 60 - color ⬭

If the answer is 70, 80, or 90 - color ⬭

$$20 + 0$$

$$20 + 30$$

$$10 + 20$$

$$20 + 20$$

$$60 + 10$$

$$40 + 40$$

$$30 + 10$$

$$50 + 10$$

$$10 + 0$$

$$10 + 10$$

$$10 + 20$$

$$30 + 30$$

$$10 + 20$$

$$10 + 30$$

$$60 + 30$$

$$50 + 20$$

$$20 + 10$$

$$20 + 40$$

$$30 + 0$$

$$40 + 10$$

$$10 + 0$$

24

MISSING ADDENDS

Color ☐ when the missing addend is 2, 3, or 4.

Color ☐ when the missing addend is 5, 6, or 7.

Color ☐ when the missing addend is 8 or 9.

$8 + \square = 10$

$6 + \square = 10$

$7 + \square = 11$

$2 + \square = 8$

$4 + \square = 12$

$7 + \square = 16$

$3 + \square = 12$

$6 + \square = 15$

$\begin{array}{r} 5 \\ +\square \\ \hline 9 \end{array}$

$\begin{array}{r} 5 \\ +\square \\ \hline 10 \end{array}$

$\begin{array}{r} 6 \\ +\square \\ \hline 12 \end{array}$

$\begin{array}{r} 4 \\ +\square \\ \hline 8 \end{array}$

$6 + \square = 14$

$10 + \square = 18$

$9 + \square = 17$

$5 + \square = 13$

$4 + \square = 11$

$1 + \square = 5$

$7 + \square = 10$

$5 + \square = 8$

25

SUBTRACTION

Color sections with answers of 6 ⬭

Color sections with answers of 7 ⬭

Color sections with answers of 8 ⬭

$$12 - 6$$

$$14 - 6$$

$$16 - 8$$

$$11 - 3$$

$$11 - 5$$

$$17 - 9$$

$$14 - 7$$

$$17 - 10$$

$$12 - 6$$

$$11 - 5$$

$$19 - 12$$

$$12 - 5$$

$$13 - 6$$

$$9 - 2$$

$$18 - 12$$

$$14 - 8$$

$$10 - 3$$

$$16 - 9$$

$$13 - 5$$

$$13 - 7$$

$$10 - 2$$

$$19 - 11$$

$$18 - 12$$

$$12 - 4$$

SUBTRACTION — NO REGROUPING

Color ⬭ when answer is 0 or 1.

Color ⬭ when answer is 2, 3, or 4.

Color ⬭ when answer is 5, 6, or 7.

Color ⬭ when answer is 8 or 9.

13-13=

10-7=

8-6=

9-4=

14-8=

10-9=

16-8=

12-11=

10-1=

12-8=

9-6=

18-9=

6-5=

16-7=

17-16=

13-7=

12-5=

7-4=

11-7=

27

8-8=

ADDITION AND SUBTRACTION

Color ☐ when the answer is 5.

Color ☐ when the answer is 6.

Color ☐ when the answer is 7.

Color ☐ when the answer is 8.

$9 - 3 =$

$\begin{array}{r} 5 \\ +2 \\ \hline \end{array}$

$\begin{array}{r} 8 \\ -1 \\ \hline \end{array}$

$7 - 1 =$

$6 - 2 =$

$8 - 4 =$

$8 - 0 =$

$3 + 2 =$

$1 + 4 =$

$6 + 2 =$

$5 + 3 =$

$6 - 1 =$

$8 - 3 =$

$9 - 1 =$

$3 + 1 =$

$5 - 1 =$

$\begin{array}{r} 4 \\ +3 \\ \hline \end{array}$

$\begin{array}{r} 9 \\ -2 \\ \hline \end{array}$

$5 + 1 =$

$8 - 2 =$

28

ADDITION and SUBTRACTION
No Regrouping

If answer is 12 - color ⬭

If answer is 13 - color ⬭

If answer is 14 - color ⬭

$$\begin{array}{r} 18 \\ -5 \\ \hline \end{array}$$

$$\begin{array}{r} 16 \\ -4 \\ \hline \end{array}$$

$$\begin{array}{r} 19 \\ -5 \\ \hline \end{array}$$

$$\begin{array}{r} 15 \\ -3 \\ \hline \end{array}$$

$$\begin{array}{r} 19 \\ -6 \\ \hline \end{array}$$

$$\begin{array}{r} 10 \\ +2 \\ \hline \end{array}$$

$$\begin{array}{r} 17 \\ -4 \\ \hline \end{array}$$

$$\begin{array}{r} 12 \\ -0 \\ \hline \end{array}$$

$$\begin{array}{r} 15 \\ -2 \\ \hline \end{array}$$

$$\begin{array}{r} 18 \\ -6 \\ \hline \end{array}$$

$$\begin{array}{r} 2 \\ 12 \\ +0 \\ \hline \end{array}$$

$$\begin{array}{r} 2 \\ +10 \\ \hline \end{array}$$

$$\begin{array}{r} 3 \\ 0 \\ 1 \\ +10 \\ \hline \end{array}$$

$$\begin{array}{r} 11 \\ +1 \\ \hline \end{array}$$

$$\begin{array}{r} 17 \\ -3 \\ \hline \end{array}$$

$$\begin{array}{r} 17 \\ -5 \\ \hline \end{array}$$

$$\begin{array}{r} 13 \\ -0 \\ \hline \end{array}$$

$$\begin{array}{r} 12 \\ +0 \\ \hline \end{array}$$

$$\begin{array}{r} 1 \\ 10 \\ +2 \\ \hline \end{array}$$

$$\begin{array}{r} 18 \\ -6 \\ \hline \end{array}$$

$$\begin{array}{r} 12 \\ +1 \\ \hline \end{array}$$

$$\begin{array}{r} 19 \\ -7 \\ \hline \end{array}$$

$$\begin{array}{r} 3 \\ 9 \\ +2 \\ \hline \end{array}$$

$$\begin{array}{r} 13 \\ -1 \\ \hline \end{array}$$

$$\begin{array}{r} 16 \\ -3 \\ \hline \end{array}$$

+ and — 3 DIGITS — REGROUPING

Work all problems - record answers - circle the number in the TENS place. Follow directions.

When the circled number is 0, 1, or 2 - color ☐.

When the circled number is 3, 4, or 5 - color ☐.

When the circled number is 6 or 7 - color ☐.

When the circled number is 8 or 9 - color ☐.

746 −237	681 − 437	983 −276
516 +247	476 −108	716 +176	993 − 308	828 +132	486 −108
219 +203	412 +229	318 + 307
444 + 546	626 +247	637 +148
318 +318	813 +138	964 −556	405 +405	812 +139	994 −135
790 −309	876 −207	635 + 256
445 −239	627 +317	454 − 327
683 −204	325 +338	885 +105	890 − 205	462 +108	293 − 117
602 + 219	573 − 218	460 − 139

ADDITION & SUBTRACTION with regrouping

Work problems - circle number in ones place.

If the circled number is 0-1-2 color ☐.

If the circled number is 3 or 4 color ☐.

If the circled number is 5 or 6 color ☐.

If the circled number is 7-8-9 color ☐.

$45 + 27 =$

$22 + 39 =$

$56 + 29 =$

$91 - 17 =$

$88 + 7 =$

$54 + 19 =$

$38 - 19 =$

$56 - 19 =$

$39 + 57 =$

$97 - 59$

$75 - 17$

$19 + 36 =$

$77 + 13$

$33 + 58$

$77 + 17 =$

$48 + 26 =$

$44 + 47$

$70 - 48$

$82 - 28 =$

$66 + 27 =$

$85 - 29 =$

$62 - 24$

$73 - 34$

$43 - 28 =$

$83 - 59 =$

$62 - 25$

$64 - 18 =$

$72 - 29 =$

$52 - 17 =$

$33 - 14$

$39 + 43 =$

$44 + 28 =$

31

ADDITION or SUBTRACTION?

Put a (+) or (—) in each ▲.

If the sign in the ▲ is (+), color ⬭

If the sign in the ▲ is (—), color ⬭

4▲3=7 2▲3=5
8▲1=7
5▲2=3
8▲5=3
5▲1=4
3▲2=5
3▲5=8

7▲5=2
6▲4=2
4▲1=5 3▲3=6
2▲5=7
8▲1=9
9▲3=6
7▲4=3

6▲2=4
3▲2=1
5▲4=9
2▲6=8
1▲6=7
5▲2=7
4▲2=2
6▲5=1

3▲1=4
2▲7=9
6▲3=3
7▲2=5
9▲4=5
6▲1=5
2▲2=4 4▲4=8

32

ADDITION & SUBTRACTION

Missing Addends

What is the missing number ● ?

When the missing number is 6 - color ☐.

When the missing number is 7 - color ☐.

When the missing number is 8 - color ☐.

When the missing number is 9 - color ☐.

$43 + ● = 49$
$37 - ● = 30$
$8 + ● = 15$
$17 + ● = 23$
$24 + ● = 32$
$44 + ● = 50$
$42 + ● = 50$
$56 - ● = 50$
$19 - ● = 11$
$47 - ● = 40$
$21 + ● = 29$
$50 - ● = 43$
$52 - ● \over 46$
$17 - ● = 9$
$35 + ● = 41$
$15 - ● = 9$
$16 - ● = 8$
$23 + ● = 30$
$16 - ● = 10$
$33 + ● = 40$
$9 + ● = 16$
$24 + ● = 31$
$18 + ● = 24$
$29 - ● \over 23$
$18 - ● \over 9$
$11 + ● \over 17$
$26 + ● = 32$
$42 - ● = 35$
$19 + ● = 26$
$21 + ● = 27$
$21 + ● = 28$
$26 - ● = 19$
$37 + ● = 43$
$82 - ● \over 76$
$41 - ● = 35$
$23 - ● = 15$
$61 + ● = 67$
$23 + ● = 31$
$41 + ● = 48$
$53 + ● = 60$
$47 - ● = 41$
$32 + ● = 40$
$16 + ● = 24$
$40 - ● = 32$
$38 - ● = 30$
$82 + ● = 88$
$18 + ● = 25$
$21 - ● = 14$
$26 + ● = 32$

33

ADDITION — 3 DIGITS — with Regrouping

Work all problems - record answers - circle number

in tens place.

If the circled number is 1, 2, or 3 - color ☐.

If the circled number is 4 or 5 - color ☐.

If the circled number is 6 or 7 - color ☐.

If the circled number is 8 or 9 - color ☐.

727
+108

417
+534

432
+108

127
+107

137
+526

347
+637

461
+429

324
+539

225
+225

205
+306

351
+819

526
+206

137
+118

524
+267

538
+233

749
+243

238
+239

128
+864

307
+185

534
+446

817
+139

715
+107

146
+325

403
+307

446
+409

318
+245

665
+217

565
+218

135
+639

519
+401

723
+127

726
+115

119
+612

ADDITION — 3 DIGITS — REGROUPING

Work all problems - record all answers - circle number in hundreds place.

When the circled number is 4 or 5 - color ☐.

When the circled number is 6 or 7 - color ☐.

When the circled number is 8 - color ☐.

When the circled number is 9 - color ☐.

281 +543	362 +146
152 +787	670 +260 366 +291	270 +488
372 +462	286 +262
195 +222	685 +193
186 +482	263 +391 282 +635	471 +461
250 +250	160 +690
255 +552	287 +171
580 +353	865 +74 541 +75	465 +260
222 +594	284 +265
360 +160	461 +393
352 +263	158 +471 643 +260	284 +684
153 +355	448 +381

35

MULTIPLICATION

Work all problems - circle number in the tens place.

If the circled number is 1 or 2 color ⬭

If the circled number is 3 or 5 color ⬭

If the circled number is 5 or 6 color ⬭

If the circled number is 7 or 8 color ⬭

If the circled number is 9 color ⬭

$7 \times 11 =$

$9 \times 8 =$

$12 \times 3 =$

$3 \times 5 =$

$9 \times 7 =$

$4 \times 12 =$

$6 \times 10 =$

$11 \times 5 =$

$10 \times 2 =$

$5 \times 10 =$

$5 \times 9 =$

$11 \times 4 =$

$9 \times 11 =$

$11 \times 3 =$

$10 \times 7 =$

$7 \times 11 =$

$9 \times 10 =$

$11 \times 2 =$

$8 \times 9 =$

$8 \times 10 =$

$6 \times 4 =$

$10 \times 9 =$

$3 \times 10 =$

$7 \times 7 =$

$11 \times 9 =$

$6 \times 8 =$

$8 \times 3 =$

$6 \times 11 =$

$8 \times 8 =$

$10 \times 5 =$

$7 \times 9 =$

$10 \times 4 =$

$4 \times 8 =$

$9 \times 2 =$

$9 \times 9 =$

$11 \times 8 =$

MISSING FACTORS

Put the missing factor in each circle.

⬤ if the missing factor is 2.
⬤ if the missing factor is 3.
⬤ if the missing factor is 4.
⬤ if the missing factor is 5.

$2 \times \bigcirc = 4$

$4 \times \bigcirc = 12$

$\bigcirc \times 2 = 6$

$\bigcirc \times 5 = 10$

$6 \times \bigcirc = 24$

$9 \times \bigcirc = 36$

$4 \times \bigcirc = 16$

$7 \times \bigcirc = 21$

$5 \times \bigcirc = 25$

$9 \times \bigcirc = 30$

$\bigcirc \times 1 = 4$

$\bigcirc \times 2 = 8$

$3 \times \bigcirc = 12$

$8 \times \bigcirc = 32$

$\bigcirc \times 2 = 8$

$3 \times \bigcirc = 9$

$8 \times \bigcirc = 40$

$9 \times \bigcirc = 27$

$7 \times \bigcirc = 35$

$\bigcirc \times 2 = 10$

$\bigcirc \times 3 = 15$

$6 \times \bigcirc = 18$

$2 \times \bigcirc = 8$

$\bigcirc \times 9 = 36$

$\bigcirc \times 3 = 12$

$1 \times \bigcirc = 4$

$\bigcirc \times 9 = 45$

$\bigcirc \times 1 = 5$

$\bigcirc \times 4 = 16$

$\bigcirc \times 5 = 20$

$5 \times \bigcirc = 20$

$\bigcirc \times 8 = 32$

$\bigcirc \times 5 = 15$

$\bigcirc \times 5 = 15$

$8 \times \bigcirc = 16$

$\bigcirc \times 1 = 3$

$8 \times \bigcirc = 24$

$\bigcirc \times 9 = 18$

37

MISSING FACTORS

If the missing factor is 2 or 3 - color ☐.

If the missing factor is 4 or 5 - color ☐.

If the missing factor is 6 or 7 - color ☐.

If the missing factor is 8 or 9 - color ☐.

$9 \times \square = 72$

$6 \times \square = 36$

$10 = \square \times 2$

$28 = \square \times 4$

$\square \times 5 = 20$

$\square \times 9 = 40$

$\square \times 7 = 14$

$4 \times \square = 24$

$25 = 5 \times \square$

$8 \times \square = 16$

$\square \times 6 = 30$

$7 \times \square = 49$

$28 = \square \times 4$

$40 = \square \times 10$

$\square \times 8 = 32$

$8 \times \square = 56$

$8 \times \square = 24$

$9 \times \square = 81$

$7 \times \square = 35$

$\square \times 3 = 18$

$\square \times 2 = 8$

$12 = 2 \times \square$

$10 = \square \times 5$

$4 \times \square = 36$

38

MISSING FACTORS

Place the missing factor in each square.

If the missing factor is 1 - color ⬭

If the missing factor is 2 - color ⬭

If the missing factor is 3 - color ⬭

If the missing factor is 4 - color ⬭

If the missing factor is 5 - color ⬭

$12 \div \square = 6$

$10 \div \square = 2$

$12 \div \square = 3$

$6 \div \square = 3$

$12 \div \square = 4$

$\square \div \square = 9$

$16 \div \square = 8$

$25 \div \square = 5$

$28 \div \square = 7$

$6 \div \square = 6$

$9 \div \square = 3$

$18 \div \square = 9$

$4 \div \square = 2$

$10 \div \square = 5$

$18 \div \square = 6$

$8 \div \square = 8$

$8 \div \square = 2$

$35 \div \square = 7$

$4 \div \square = 2$

$4 \div \square = 4$

$15 \div \square = 5$

$14 \div \square = 7$

$20 \div \square = 5$

$45 \div \square = 9$

$2 \div \square = 1$

39

READING & MATH BOOKS by JOHN H. LETTAU

1st Dimension	Grades 3-6
2nd Dimension	Grades 3-6
Primary Dimension	Grades 1-4
Aztec Math Primary Book One	Grades 1-3
Aztec Math Primary Book Two	Grades 1-3
Aztec Math Intermediate Book One	Grades 3-6
Aztec Math Intermediate Book Two	Grades 3-6
Aztec Math Jr. High Book One	Grades 5-8
Aztec Math Jr. High Book Two	Grades 5-8
Aztec Math Decimal Book	Grades 4-8
Aztec Math Fraction Book	Grades 4-8
Sum-Action Number Puzzle Book One	Grades 3-6
Sum-Action Number Puzzle Book Two	Grades 3-6
Sum-Action Number Puzzle Primary Book One	Grades 1-3
Sum-Action Number Puzzle Primary Book Two	Grades 1-3
Multiplication Number Puzzles	Grades 3-6
Geometric Design Puzzle Book One	Grades 3-6
Geometric Design Puzzle Book Two	Grades 3-6
Aztec Reading Primary Book One	Grades 1-3
Aztec Reading Primary Book Two	Grades 1-3
Math in Action	Grades 3-6
A-Maze-ing Number Puzzles	Grades 3-6
Graph Paper Designs	Grades 2-6
Pick-A-Dilly Papers	Grades 3-6
Awards for All Reasons	Grades 1-6
Time Marches On	Grades 1-3
Pennies, Nickels & Dimes	Grades 1-3
Super-Sum Activity Cards	Grades 3-6
Learning Center Game Boards	Grades 1-3
Aztec Design Coloring Book	Grades 1-6

Made in the USA
Las Vegas, NV
03 July 2021